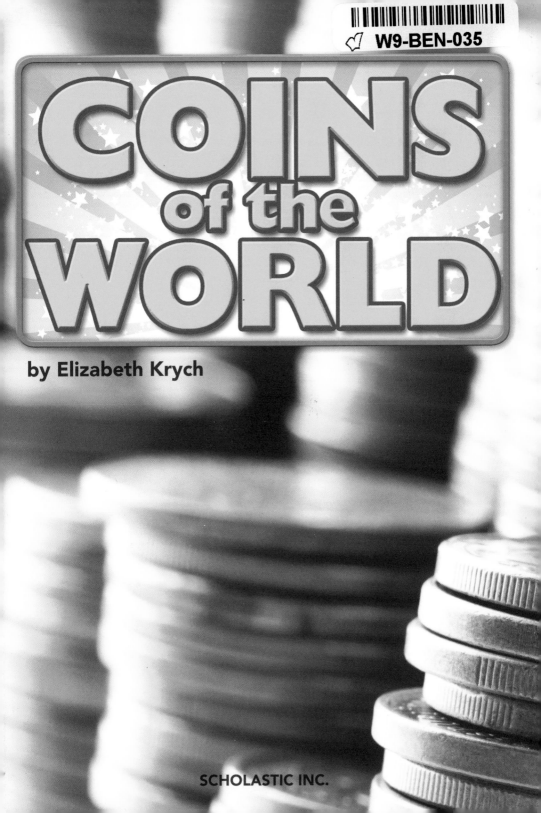

COINS of the WORLD

by Elizabeth Krych

SCHOLASTIC INC.

For Dave -E. K.

ISBN: 978-0-545-69224-3
Copyright © 2015 by Scholastic Inc.
All rights reserved. Published by Scholastic Inc., Publishers since 1920. SCHOLASTIC and associated logos are trademarks and/or registered trademarks of Scholastic Inc.

12 11 10 9 8 7 6 5 4 3 2 1   15 16 17 18/0
Book design by Maria Mercado
Photo research by Alan Gottlieb
First printing, February 2015

Printed in China   95

CONTENTS

INTRODUCTION

Coins are easy to carry in your pocket, use in vending machines, and save in a piggy bank. But those jingling, shiny disks have a lot more to say than just heads or tails! Look closer, and you'll quickly see that coins can be fun and fascinating to collect.

The story of coins began a few thousand years ago, when people used small amounts of valuable metals, measured by weight, to buy and sell things. But over time, this system became confusing. So about 2,700 years ago, people started to make coins. They were easier to handle and had an agreed-upon value.

In Lydia (located in present-day Turkey), early coins were very small and lumpy. In China, the first coins were made of bronze and looked like small, flat tools. A few centuries later, round coins of the Greek and Roman empires showed a face on one side and symbols and the value on the other. Many objects were used as money in different parts of the world, but this Roman style was eventually used everywhere.

Funny money

All these items have been used as money in different parts of the world. Imagine carrying this change in your pocket!

- Salt, sugar, tea, and cocoa beans
- Seashells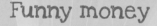
- Wild dogs' teeth
- Gold dust
- Parrot feathers
- Jawbones of giant bats
- Round pieces of limestone weighing up to 2,000 pounds

The ancient Chinese added a square hole to their tool-shaped coins so they could be tied together. Eventually, coins became just disks with a square hole.

The ancient Greek empire (circa 750 – 200 BCE) put images of gods, goddesses, and heroes on its coins, as well as symbols for different cities. Early Roman coins (circa 300 BCE) copied Greek designs, but later on they showed portraits of Roman leaders. These coins traveled throughout the Roman Empire across Europe, Asia, and parts of Africa. Many symbols on modern coins come from these ancient designs.

Today, all countries use a mixture of paper money and coins, called **currency**. The central bank of each country (or group of countries) is in charge of making and keeping track of currency. Coins are made in a factory called a **mint**. The process of making coins is also called "minting." When an economy suffers from **inflation**, the central bank sometimes makes money with larger values, or creates a whole new system of currency.

The United States Mint has been making coins since 1792. Today there are four mints, in Denver, San Francisco, West Point, and Philadelphia.

Weimar hyperinflation

Coins were originally made of gold, silver, and other precious metals, so they were valuable in themselves. Over time, cheaper metals and paper money were introduced. This currency has a "face value" set by the government. For a year during the Weimar Republic in Germany (1922–1923), the government tried to help the economy by printing more and more paper money. The plan failed because there was now so much money that it was almost worthless. The government tried to keep up by printing "fifty thousand" and then "fifty million" mark notes (above left). But you still had to have piles of cash just to buy bread!

Most coins today are smaller and lighter than they used to be. They are made from cheaper materials, like steel and aluminum, to lower production costs.

Counterfeiting

Criminals have probably been making **counterfeit**–fake–coins ever since coins were invented. Many coins have been redesigned in the past few years to make them harder to copy. Common changes include using two different types of metal, laser engraving, and micro-writing. Paper money has added holograms, watermarks, and special inks. It is much harder for these details to be faked, but the U.S. Secret Service is always on the lookout, as are other organizations around the world.

Looking at coins from different places in history can tell us a lot about what was going on at that time. Different pictures and writing show changes in rulers and governments.

Argentine hyperinflation

Toward the end of the twentieth century, Argentina tried to fix its inflation problem by changing its entire currency system. In 1970, the government introduced the peso ley to replace the old national peso. In 1983, these were traded in for the Argentine peso. Two years later, the austral became the official currency—before switching to yet another kind of peso in 1992.

When you look at a coin, keep in mind that every little detail has been created for a reason. The shape, pictures, and writing give clues about the people who use it and what they value. Here are some things to look for as you start your coin collection.

OBVERSE/"HEADS"

LEGEND/MOTTO

PORTRAIT (PRESIDENT ABRAHAM LINCOLN)

DATE OF MINTING

INITIALS OF ARTIST

REVERSE/"TAILS"

NAME OF COUNTRY

LEGEND/MOTTO IN LATIN

NATIONAL FLAG OR SYMBOL

VALUE

INITIALS OF ARTIST

INITIALS OF ARTIST

Shape, size, and edge: Not all coins are round! A coin can be a polygon, have a wavy rim, or even have a hole through the middle. The edge of a coin may be smooth, ridged, patterned, or engraved with a message.

Obverse: The obverse is often the "heads" side, but there is no fixed rule about which side is which.

Date: Usually the year the coin was made. Some cultures count years differently than the U.S. does.

Portrait: The person shown might be the current ruler, a former leader, a famous person from history, or a symbolic face that isn't a real person at all.

Reverse: The "tails" side usually shows the value and a picture or symbol.

Legend: Many coins have writing in more than one language or more than one alphabet.

Tiny letters: Very small letters on a coin can be a mint mark (showing where it was made) or the initials of the designer. "Micro-writing" can only be read with a magnifying glass. This makes coins hard to counterfeit.

Symbols and images: In addition to important people, many coins show animals, plants, artwork, or buildings that are special to their countries of origin. Many kinds of symbols are also used.

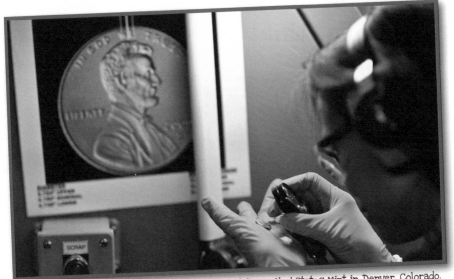

Press operator inspects a freshly minted penny at the United States Mint in Denver, Colorado.

People have been collecting coins almost as long as they have been making them. Studying and collecting coins is called **numismatics**. You don't need any special equipment to start a coin collection, just curiosity and patience.

This book shows more than 30 modern coins from around the world. The coins were chosen to show the variety of money in use worldwide. Each page gives a close-up look at the coin's design, with some information about where it comes from. The central bank for each currency is also given. Most central banks and mints have websites in English with a lot more information. More online resources are given on page 48. The value of most coins described in this book was 50 cents or less at the time of writing.

You can begin your numismatic collection in the clear pockets in the back of this book. Get started by just looking through your own pocket change. You could collect the 50 state quarters or the National Parks quarters series. Or you could try to find a penny from every year in the last 100 years! If you know someone who travels overseas, you could ask them nicely to bring you back some small change.

Happy collecting!

Countries in this book:

The maps below show the countries featured in this book, highlighted in color.
Get ready to explore!

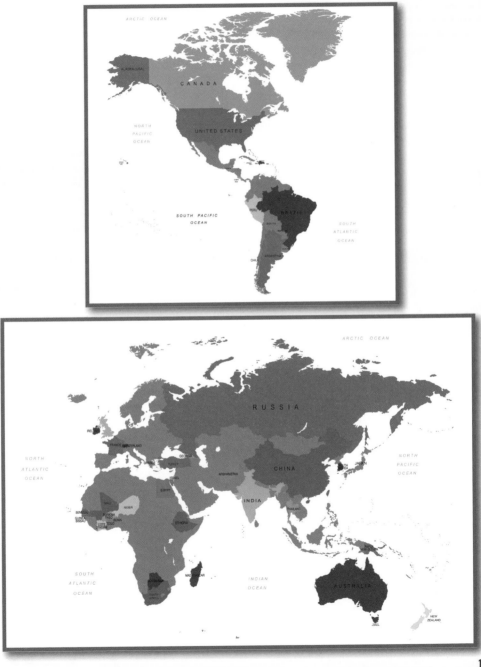

BOTSWANA

Capital: **Gaborone**
Currency: **Botswana pula**
Central Bank: **Bank of Botswana, Gaborone**
Coin: **25 thebe**
First Issued: **1976**

GABORONE

Left: Three Burchell's zebras drinking water at Makgadikgadi Pans National Park, Boteti River, Botswana.

The names of many currencies mean something valuable in the local language. When Botswana created its own money in the 1970s, the word "pula" was chosen because it means "rain" and "blessing." Botswana is a hot and dry country, so rainwater is very valuable there! One pula is equal to 100 thebe. "Thebe" means "shield."

Obverse: National **coat of arms** of a shield and two zebras.

Reverse: A zebu and the word "Ipelegeng," which means "self-improvement" in the Setswana language.

EGYPT

Capital: Cairo
Currency: Egyptian pound
Central Bank: Central Bank of Egypt, Cairo
Coin: 1 pound
First Issued: 2005

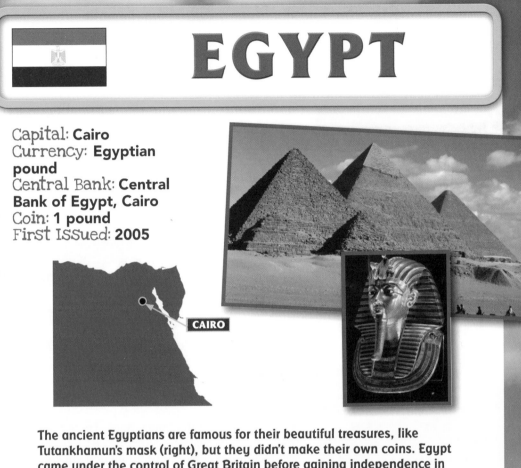

CAIRO

The ancient Egyptians are famous for their beautiful treasures, like Tutankhamun's mask (right), but they didn't make their own coins. Egypt came under the control of Great Britain before gaining independence in 1922 and borrowed the British term, pound, for its currency. Coins and paper money of Egypt show many of its famous ancient landmarks.

Obverse: The mask of Pharaoh Tutankhamun's mummy, buried in 1327 BCE and dug up in 1922. The border is an ancient Egyptian water lily design.

Reverse: The value in English and Arabic. "Arab Republic of Egypt" written in Arabic. The date is given in both the Islamic and Western calendars.

13

ETHIOPIA

Capital: Addis Ababa
Currency: Ethiopian birr
Central Bank: National Bank of Ethiopia, Addis Ababa
Coin: 1 birr
First Issued: 2010

ADDIS ABABA

Top: A monolithic rock-cut church in Lalibela

Left: A coffee farmer turns the beans as they dry in the sun, Choche, Ethiopia.

The inhabitants of the lands that became Ethiopia have been minting coins since 100 BCE or so. This coin recently replaced a 1-birr bill that showed the face of a smiling boy (left). The new coins will last much longer than paper bills.

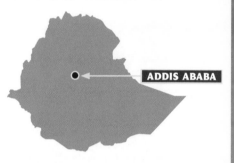

Obverse: A roaring lion, a national symbol of the country's strength.

Reverse: A balanced scale, a symbol for fairness and justice. The value of the coin and the year are written in Ethiopia's unique Amharic language.

MADAGASCAR

Capital: **Antananarivo**
Currency: **Malagasy ariary**
Central Bank: **Central Bank of Madagascar, Antananarivo**
Coin: **50 ariary**
First Issued: **2005**

ANTANANARIVO

This island nation off the southeast coast of Africa is famous for its unique wildlife, but its money is also unusual. Madagascar is one of only two countries with non-**decimal** currency, which means that 1 ariary can't be divided into 10 or 100 parts. Instead, 1 ariary is divided into 5 iraimbilanja.

Obverse: The coin's value and "Republic of Madagascar" in Malagasy.

Reverse: The Avenue of the Baobabs, a famous road lined with tall baobab trees (above), and the national motto in Malagasy, translated: "Fatherland, Liberty, Progress."

SOUTH AFRICA

Capitals: **Pretoria (executive), Bloemfontein (judicial), and Cape Town (legislative)**
Currency: **South African Rand**
Central Bank: **South African Reserve Bank, Pretoria**
Coin: **5 Rand**
First Issued: **2004**

PRETORIA

BLOEMFONTEIN

CAPE TOWN

Above: A portrait of former president and Nobel Peace Prize winner Nelson Mandela (1918-2013) is on all South African bills.

The name of South Africa's money comes from the Witwatersrand Mountains, where a lot of gold was found by European settlers in the 1800s. This **bimetallic** coin (made of two different metals) was redesigned to make it harder to counterfeit.

Obverse: The national coat of arms and the words "South Africa" in two of the eleven official languages. Every year, the languages on the coins change. This coin from 2004 uses the siSwati and Xitsonga languages.

Reverse: A charging gnu and the coin's value. The micro-writing around the gnu is the letters SARB (South African Reserve Bank), an anti-counterfeiting detail.

16

WEST AFRICAN ECONOMIC AND MONETARY UNION

Countries: **Benin, Burkina Faso, Côte d'Ivoire (Ivory Coast), Guinea-Bissau, Mali, Niger, Senegal, and Togo**
Currency: **West African CFA franc**
Central Bank: **Central Bank of West African States, Dakar, Senegal**
Coin: **200 CFA francs**
First Issued: **2003**

Above: Men playing African percussion instruments, in Burkina Faso

Right: Betammaribe house with granary, Benin

SENEGAL
MALI
NIGER
GUINEA-BISSAU
BENIN
IVORY COAST
BURKINA FASO
TOGO

Parts of central and western Africa were taken over by France in the 1800s and began to use the French franc. In 1945, France created a new currency just for this region, called the CFA franc. Eight countries in western Africa kept the currency after becoming independent a few years later. Six other nations use the Central African CFA franc.

Obverse: Asante gold dust weight (shaped like a sawfish) and "Central Bank of West African States" in French.

Reverse: Typical crops and "West African Monetary Union" in French.

17

AFGHANISTAN

Capital: Kabul
Currency: Afghan afghani
Central Bank: Da Afghanistan Bank, Kabul
Coin: 5 afghani
First Issued: 2005

KABUL

Far right: An Afghan vendor waits for customers to sell pomegranates at a market in Kandahar.

Right: Pastry shop in Afghanistan

For religious reasons, coins made in many Muslim regions do not show living things, only writing, shapes, and designs. After Afghanistan created its own currency, the afghani, in 1925, its money has shown a western-style coat of arms as well as Islamic symbols and religious messages.

Obverse: The national coat of arms, showing a mosque and a religious message in Arabic.

Reverse: The central symbol is the numeral 5 in Arabic. In smaller writing is the name of the Central Bank and the year the coin was minted.

CHINA

Capital: Beijing
Currency: Renminbi, which means "money of the people." The main unit is the yuan, divided into 10 jiao and 100 fen.
Central Bank: People's Bank of China, Beijing
Coin: 1 jiao
First Issued: 1999

BEIJING

When money is given as a gift in China, it's traditionally wrapped in a lucky red envelope.

China has some of the oldest coins in the world. A round coin with a square hole, called "cash," was used for nearly 2,000 years! Today, all small amounts are issued as both notes and coins.

Obverse: Orchids symbolize beauty and success in Chinese culture. The words translate to "People's Bank of China."

Reverse: "People's Bank of China" written in Chinese characters.

INDIA

Capital: **New Delhi**
Currency: **Indian rupee**
Central Bank: **Reserve Bank of India, New Delhi**
Coin: **10 rupee**
First Issued: **2011**

NEW DELHI

Above: The Taj Mahal

Left: Lines of yellow Ambassador taxicabs and buses in Calcutta, India

The large area of the Indian subcontinent was once divided into hundreds of small kingdoms, each with their own gold, silver, and copper coins.

Obverse: Three lions from the top of the pillars of Ashoka in Sarnath, built by King Ashoka around 250 BCE. This statue is a national symbol of India. The writing says "India" in English and Bengali.

Reverse: Ten rays symbolize prosperity. Above the number 10 is the new rupee symbol, chosen in 2010.

ISRAEL

Capital: Jerusalem
Currency: Israeli new sheqel
Central Bank: Bank of Israel, Jerusalem
Coin: 2 sheqelim
First Issued: 1986

JERUSALEM

Above: A bazaar in Old City offers traditional Middle Eastern products and souvenirs. It is a very popular site with tourists and pilgrims visiting Jerusalem.

Right: A dreidel and gelt

In 1986, when the new sheqel went into effect, the designer based the new coins on very old ones. The design on the 2-sheqelim coin dates back to the second century BCE.

Obverse: The number 2 and "Israel" in Arabic, English, and Hebrew.

Reverse: Ancient symbols of fruit, grain, and pearls displayed in two cornucopias. (We use this "horn of plenty" symbol in the U.S. as a Thanksgiving decoration.)

JAPAN

Capital: **Tokyo**
Currency: **Japanese yen**
Central Bank: **Bank of Japan, Tokyo**
Coin: **50 yen**
First Issued: **1967**

TOKYO

Money doesn't grow on trees, but many coins display trees and flowers. Some plants are national symbols, such as the Canadian maple leaf and the Irish shamrock. Here are some other plants with special meanings:

laurel leaves: victory
lotus flower: truth, peace
oak leaves: strength
palm branch: victory, peace

The modern Japanese yen goes back to the 1870s, when the Meiji Emperor decided to make his country as modern as possible. Japanese emperors are traditionally believed to be too holy to show on currency.

Obverse: Chrysanthemum flowers, a symbol of royalty and long life. The Japanese writing says "Japan, 50 yen."

Reverse: Below the number 50, the year is given in Japanese terms, dating from the reign of the emperor. This coin with the number 63 is from the sixty-third year of the former emperor's reign, or 1988.

SINGAPORE

Capital: **Singapore**
Currency: **Singapore dollar**
Central Bank: **Monetary Authority of Singapore, Singapore**
Coin: **50 cents**
First Issued: **2013**

Above: Aerial view of Singapore

Left: Locals at a popular food hall in Singapore

Singapore

Singapore is a tiny but powerful island city surrounded by Malaysia and Indonesia. It was founded as a trading post by British merchants in 1819 and has been independent since 1965. Singapore's location along a major trade route has made it a world leader in banking and shipping.

Obverse: The same design is used on all coins and says "Singapore" in the four official languages: Malay, Mandarin Chinese, English, and Tamil. The coat of arms is held up by a lion and a tiger, and the national motto translates as "Onward, Singapore!"

Reverse: The stylized lion head at top left is a symbol of Singapore and is shown on all the new coin designs. Above the value are a crane and ship that symbolize the Port of Singapore, one of the busiest shipping centers in the world.

SOUTH KOREA

Capital: Seoul
Currency: South Korean won
Central Bank: Bank of Korea, Seoul
Coin: 500 won
First Issued: 1982

SEOUL

Like many Asian currencies, Korean coins show simple images of plants, animals, and places that have special meaning in the Buddhist religion, rather than national symbols.

Obverse: A red-crested white crane, a symbol of long life and peace, and "Five Hundred Won" in Korean.

Reverse: The year of minting in Western numerals, and "Bank of Korea" in Korean.

THAILAND

Capital: Bangkok
Currency: Thai baht
Central Bank: Bank of Thailand, Bangkok
Coin: 10 baht
First Issued: 2008

BANGKOK

Right: Thailand's Queen Sirikit (C), Crown Prince Maha Vajiralongkorn (L), and Princess Chulabhorn (R)

After several centuries of oval-shaped, silver currency nicknamed "tiger tongues," the king of Thailand received a British coin-making machine from Queen Victoria in 1859 as a gift. The country has used round coins ever since.

Obverse: King Bhumibol Adulyadej, who has reigned for more than 67 years.

Reverse: The Wat Arun (Temple of Dawn), shown above, is a Buddhist temple in Bangkok. The writing on the coin is in Thai, and the year is given according to the Thai calendar. The Braille symbol for "10" is at the top.

25

AUSTRALIA

Capital: **Canberra**
Currency: **Australian dollar**
Central Bank: **Reserve Bank of Australia, Sydney**
Coin: **1 dollar**
First Issued: **1984**

CANBERRA

From 1823 to 1901, Australia was a colony of Great Britain and it used the British money, called pounds and pence. A new money system was created in 1966 of dollars and cents. At the time, some people suggested the currency should be called the royal, the austral, or the kanga!

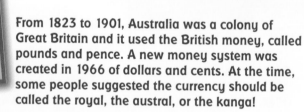

Obverse: Queen Elizabeth II of Great Britain. The current picture came into use in 1999.

Reverse: Australia's most famous animals, kangaroos.

FIJI

Capital: Suva
Currency: Fijian dollar
Central Bank: Reserve Bank of Fiji, Suva
Coin: 20 cents
First Issued: 2013

SUVA

Sometimes what is *not* shown on a coin can send a powerful message. For 78 years, the coins of Fiji showed the British monarch. But after a government change in 2009, Fiji left the British Commonwealth. A new set of coins was introduced in 2013—without the queen.

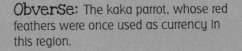

Obverse: The kaka parrot, whose red feathers were once used as currency in this region.

Reverse: A traditional whale's tooth necklace called a *tabua*.

NEW ZEALAND

Capital: **Wellington**
Currency: **New Zealand dollar**
Central Bank: **Reserve Bank of New Zealand, Wellington**
Coin: **20 cents**
First Issued: **2006**

WELLINGTON

The native people of New Zealand are the Maori. Like Australia, New Zealand was colonized by Great Britain in the 1800s. Today, its coins show images from both cultures.

Obverse: Queen Elizabeth II of Great Britain.

Reverse: A Maori statue called a *pukaki* and Maori designs.

PAPUA NEW GUINEA

Capital: Port Moresby
Currency: Papua New Guinean kina
Central Bank: Bank of Papua New Guinea, Port Moresby
Coin: 1 kina
First Issued: 1975

PORT MORESBY

When Papua New Guinea became independent from Australia in 1975, it created a new currency that comes from a word for "shell." Many people in this island nation still live in traditional villages. Over 800 languages are spoken here!

Obverse: Papua New Guinean crocodiles, which can grow to be 11 feet long!

Reverse: The bird of paradise, which is a national symbol.

EUROPEAN UNION

The Euro

Bank: European Central Bank, Frankfurt am Main, Germany
Coins: 1 euro (Greece), 5 euro cents (Ireland), 10 euro cents (France)
First Issued: 2002

Right: European Central Bank in Frankfurt, Germany

After the fall of the Soviet Union in 1991 and the end of the Cold War, many countries of Europe formed a group called the European Union. They decided to create a single currency for all countries, the euro, which most EU countries now use. This makes business and travel between countries much easier.

Member Nations

IRELAND

FRANCE

GREECE

This map represents the countries that are using the euro as of 2014.

All euro coins with the same value have the same obverse, but each country has its own set of reverse designs. Each country represents itself in a different way.

GREECE

The 1 euro reverse is based on an ancient Greek coin, used 460–290 BCE, called a tetradrachm. The old coin says "Athens" in Greek; the new coin says "1 euro."

IRELAND

All Irish coins show a harp, a symbol of Irish music and culture. The word "Eire" means "Ireland" in the Irish Gaelic language.

FRANCE

In 1789, when the French people overthrew their king and queen, symbols of freedom replaced royal designs on the coins. One famous symbol is a beautiful young woman, nicknamed "Marianne," who is planting seeds of peace and success on France's 10-euro-cents coin.

Left: A Celtic harp

Changing Change

Until 2002, every nation in Europe had its own money, including:

Belgium: Belgian franc
Estonia: Estonian kroon
Finland: Finnish markkas
Germany: German mark
Greece: Greek drachma
Netherlands: Dutch guilder
Spain: Spanish peseta

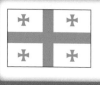

GEORGIA

Capital: **Tbilisi**
Currency: **Georgian lari**
Central Bank: **National Bank of Georgia, Tbilisi**
Coin: **20 tetri**
First Issued: **1993**

Above: Shopping at the central food market in Tbilisi, Georgia

Left: The stern profile of communist leader V.I. Lenin (1870-1924) was a familiar sight on Soviet money.

TBILISI

In 1991, the huge USSR broke apart, and use of the Soviet ruble currency ended. Newly independent countries used their new currency to celebrate their culture and history. For example, images on Georgian coins are based on works of art by Georgian artists.

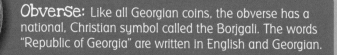

Obverse: Like all Georgian coins, the obverse has a national, Christian symbol called the Borjgali. The words "Republic of Georgia" are written in English and Georgian.

Reverse: A deer from a painting by a Georgian artist, Niko Pirosmani (1862–1918). The Georgian word at its feet is "tetri," a word adopted from the term to describe coins in ancient and medieval Georgia.

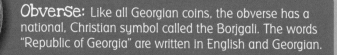

RUSSIA

Capital: Moscow
Currency: Russian ruble
Central Bank: Bank of Russia, Moscow
Coin: 10 ruble
First Issued: 2007

MOSCOW

Far right: Saint Basil's Cathedral on the Red Square, Moscow

Right: Iceberg Skating Palace, Sochi, Russia, the figure-skating venue of the 2014 Winter Olympics

The Bank of Russia uses the 10-ruble coin to show different places and events in history, like the U.S. Mint does with American quarters. Different designs are used almost every year.

Obverse: The inside of the 0 in the number 10 is laser engraved. If you tilt the coin one way, you can see "10," and tilted the other way, it says "rubles." This hidden writing is supposed to be very hard to counterfeit.

Reverse: Coat of arms of Rostovskaya Oblast. There are 46 oblasts, or provinces, in Russia.

✚ SWITZERLAND

Capital: **Bern**
Currency: **Swiss franc**
Central Bank: **Bank of Switzerland, Bern**
Coin: **1/2 franc**
First Issued: **1879**

BERN

Snowy, mountainous Switzerland is known for safety and politeness, which is why it is one of the world headquarters of banking. Although it is surrounded by countries that use the euro, it holds on to its Swiss francs!

Obverse: A woman with a spear and a shield wearing a Roman dress, to symbolize the country's long history. "Helvetia" is the name for Switzerland in Latin, the ancient Roman language. The 23 stars represent the 23 Swiss cantons (provinces).

Reverse: The oak leaves on the left symbolize wisdom and strength. The mountain leaves and flowers on the right are found in the Swiss Alps.

TURKEY

Capital: **Ankara**
Currency: **Turkish lira**
Central Bank: **Central Bank
of the Republic of Turkey, Ankara**
Coin: **50 kuru**
First Issued: **2009**

ANKARA

Turkey selected a new symbol for the lira in 2012, out of more than 8,000 entries in a national contest. The winning design looks like an anchor, symbolizing stability and progress.

Top: Bosphorus Bridge in Istanbul

Above: Turkish slippers

Obverse: The Bosphorus Bridge, which connects the two sides of Istanbul and also joins Europe and Asia, and a bird's-eye view of the Bosphorus Strait. The crescent and star symbol is on the Turkish flag.

Reverse: All Turkish coins show nationalist leader and first president, Mustafa Kemal Atatürk (1881–1938).

⊞ UNITED KINGDOM

Capital: London
Currency: British pound sterling
Central Bank: Bank of England, London
Coin: 20 pence
First Issued: 2008

LONDON

Although the United Kingdom's laws are made by an elected Parliament, who meet in the Palace of Westminster (top), the nation also has a royal family, including Prince Charles (born 1948) and Queen Elizabeth II (born 1926), pictured above.

The obverse of British coins shows the current king or queen in profile, looking the opposite way from the monarch that came before him or her. Queen Elizabeth II has been on the money since 1953. When her son Prince Charles becomes king, he will be shown looking left.

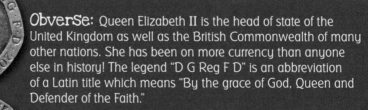

Obverse: Queen Elizabeth II is the head of state of the United Kingdom as well as the British Commonwealth of many other nations. She has been on more currency than anyone else in history! The legend "D G Reg F D" is an abbreviation of a Latin title which means "By the grace of God, Queen and Defender of the Faith."

Reverse: This unusual picture is part of a puzzle. When you put the reverses of British coins together, they make up the royal coat of arms.

CANADA

Capital: **Ottawa**
Currency: **Canadian dollar**
Central Bank: **Bank of Canada, Ottawa**
Coin: **1 dollar coin**
First Issued: **1987**

OTTAWA

The one-dollar coin is called a "loonie" by Canadians; the two-dollar coin is known as a "toonie"! The dollar coin replaced a dollar bill in 1987. The Royal Candian Mint was founded in 1908 to process Canadian gold. Today it mints coins for Canada and also for many other countries.

Top: Quebec city skyline in autumn

Above: Canada Day celebration in the front of British Columbia's Parliament Building

Obverse: Queen Elizabeth II of Great Britain. This portrait came into use in 2003.

Reverse: The common loon, found across Canada. A laser mark with a maple leaf above the loon is a security feature.

COSTA RICA

Capital: **San José**
Currency: **Costa Rican colón**
Central Bank: **Central Bank of Costa Rica, San José**
Coin: **500 colones**
First Issued: **2003**

SAN JOSE

Top: A worker selects coffee berries, at a farm in Santa Maria de Dota

Left: Arenal Volcano in La Fortuna, Costa Rica

The colón is named after Christopher Columbus (Cristóbal Colón in Spanish). Very few people have an entire currency named for them! Others include the balboa (Panama, explorer Vasco de Balboa), and the bolívar (Venezuela, revolutionary Simón Bolívar).

Obverse: The coat of arms of Costa Rica has beans on the sides that represent coffee beans, a major crop.

Reverse: The value in numbers and Braille, and the initials of the bank's name in Spanish.

GUATEMALA

Capital: **Guatemala City**
Currency: **Guatemalan quetzal**
Central Bank: **Bank of Guatemala, Guatemala City**
Coin: **1 quetzal**
First Issued: **2000**

GUATEMALA CITY

In 1925, the currency of Guatemala changed to a new form named after the national bird, the quetzal, which has been an important symbol in this region since the days of the Aztecs.

Birds on Coins

Birds are shown on coins both realistically and as symbols. Here are some more birds with special meanings.

eagle: strength, independence (USA)
owl: wisdom (Greece)
peacock: queens (ancient Rome)
rooster: the people of France
sparrow: faith, hope (South Africa)

Obverse: The Guatemalan coat of arms, including a quetzal bird and the date September 15, 1821, when the nation became independent from Spain. The year of minting is below.

Reverse: Along with a dove of peace is the date December 29, 1996, and "stable and lasting peace" in Spanish. This date marked the end of a long civil war.

JAMAICA

Capital: Kingston
Currency: Jamaican dollar
Central Bank: Bank of Jamaica, Kingston
Coin: 10 dollars
First Issued: 1999

KINGSTON

As a colony, Jamaica used Spanish currency, and then British. After independence in 1962, Jamaica's money was still based on the design of British currency and showed the British monarch. Finally, in 1969, Jamaica rolled out a new decimal currency of dollars and cents with portraits of national heroes.

Obverse: Jamaica's coat of arms features two native Taino people and a crocodile.

Reverse: George Gordon (1820–1865) was a politician and businessman who encouraged Jamaicans to resist injustice.

DOMINICAN REPUBLIC

Capital: **Santo Domingo**
Currency: **Dominican peso**
Central Bank: **Central Bank of Dominican Republic, Santo Domingo**
Coin: **25 pesos**
First Issued: **2005**

SANTO DOMINGO

The Dominican Republic shares an island in the Caribbean Sea with Haiti, and was visited by Christopher Columbus in 1492. After many years as a Spanish colony, it kept a Spanish name for its currency. Sugar and coffee are grown there, and the beautiful beaches are popular with tourists. Today, many Major League Baseball players come from the Dominican Republic.

Top: Dancers parading at Carnival

Above: Coat of arms of the Dominican Republic

Obverse: Gregorio Luperón (1839–1897), a nationalist leader and president, along with the year of minting and the name of the central bank in Spanish.

Reverse: The value and "Dominican Republic," with the national coat of arms.

UNITED STATES OF AMERICA

Capital: **Washington, D.C.**
Currency: **United States dollar**
Central Bank: **Federal Reserve, Washington, D.C.**
Coin: **5 cents**
First Issued: **2006**

Thomas Jefferson (1743–1826) started planning America's money even before the U.S. declared independence from Great Britain in 1776. When Jefferson first appeared on five-cent coins, they were called "half dimes" and were made out of silver. When the metal changed to a mixture of nickel and copper, people started calling them nickels.

Obverse: This view of the third president is the first American obverse that is not in profile. "Liberty" is in Jefferson's own handwriting. The letter beneath the date is the mint mark.

Reverse: Jefferson's house, Monticello, has been shown on nickels since 1938. The Latin words above the house mean "Out of many, one." This motto dates back to 1776.

The fifty states and several American territories use the U.S. dollar today, but did you know that many other currencies were used in the past?

Massachusetts

Defying a charter from England, the Massachusetts Bay Colony set up a mint in 1652. They mainly created shillings, valued at 12 pence.

WASHINGTON D.C.

Texas

After independence from Mexico, Texas was a republic from 1836 to 1845. Millions of "star money" and "redback" dollars were printed in Houston, but no Texan coins were ever made.

Hawaii

The Hawaiian Islands were an independent kingdom until 1893. In the 1800s, Hawaii's coins showed its kings and queens.

Capital: Buenos Aires
Currency: Argentine peso
Central Bank: Central Bank
of the Republic of Argentina,
Buenos Aires
Coin: 50 centavos
First Issued: 1992

BUENOS AIRES

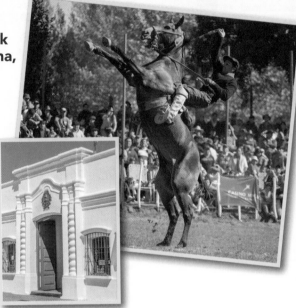

"Argentina" comes from the word meaning "silver" in Latin. Its silver mines were a source of great wealth for Spain when Argentina was a colony. Argentina is famous for its cows and cowboys, called gauchos (above).

Obverse: The words "Argentine Republic in Union and Liberty" in Spanish surround the House of Independence (above), where Argentina's declaration of independence was signed in 1816.

Reverse: The value and year of minting.

BRAZIL

Capital: **Brasília**
Currency: **Brazilian real
(plural: reis)**
Central Bank: **Central
Bank of Brazil, Brasília**
Coin: **1 real**
First Issued: **1998**

BRASILIA

Brazil has a lot of gold and silver. In the 1690s, Portuguese and Spanish colonizers built mines and mints to make real ("royal") coins. For part of the twentieth century, Brazil changed to a new currency called the cruzeiro, from the Portuguese word for the Southern Cross constellation, but the "real" name returned in 1994.

Obverse: This imaginary woman is a symbol of Brazil. The border pattern on both sides is based on native folk art.

Reverse: The stars in the center are the Southern Cross, a constellation seen in the Southern Hemisphere.

CHILE

Capital: **Santiago**
Currency: **Chilean peso**
Central Bank: **Central Bank of Chile, Santiago**
Coin: **100 pesos**
First Issued: **1984**

SANTIAGO →

Chile is a skinny, mountainous country with a lot of copper, and the 100-peso coin is almost solid copper, which is tinted two different colors. The coat of arms of Chile features a mountain bird, the Andean condor. This huge vulture with a ten-foot wingspan is also the symbol of Chile's Central Bank.

Obverse: An image of a Mapuche woman, the native people of Chile.

Reverse: Chile's coat of arms has a small deer called a huemul on the left and an Andean condor on the right. The edge of the coin is surrounded by laurel leaves, an ancient Greek symbol of victory.

PERU

Capital: **Lima**
Currency: **Peruvian nuevo sol**
Central Bank: **Central Reserve Bank of Peru, Lima**
Coin: **20 centimos**
First Issued: **1991**

Top: Machu Picchu

Left: Children in traditional clothing play with animals.

LIMA

Peru's nuevo sol ("new sun") currency replaced the inti, which was named after the Incan sun god. Before the inti, the currency was called sol de oro ("golden sun").

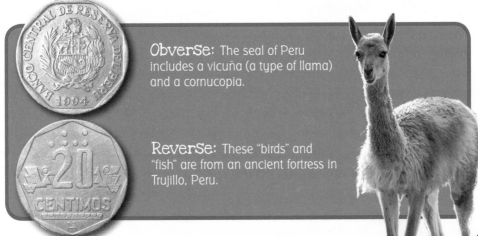

Obverse: The seal of Peru includes a vicuña (a type of llama) and a cornucopia.

Reverse: These "birds" and "fish" are from an ancient fortress in Trujillo, Peru.

GLOSSARY

bimetallic: made of two different kinds of metal

coat of arms: a group of symbols used to represent a country; also called an emblem or seal

counterfeit: fake, or the act of making something fake

currency: objects officially used as money

decimal: can be divided by ten

inflation: an increase in the price of goods and services in an economy that makes money worth less than usual

legend: the writing on a coin

mint: a place where coins are made, or the act of making coins

motto: a short statement that sums up something or someone's beliefs

numismatics: the act of collecting or studying coins

obverse: the front of a coin, often showing a person or a coat of arms, called "heads"

portrait: a picture of a person

profile: a side view of a person's face

reverse: the back side of a coin, often showing the value and a symbol, called "tails"

For further information
U.S. Mint Kids: History in Your Pocket
www.usmint.gov/kids/

National Numismatic Collection of the Smithsonian Institution
www.americanhistory.si.edu/numismatics/

Coin Collection of the British Museum, London
www.britishmuseum.org/explore/themes/money.aspx